The Unexpected Journey

Living on the Edge of Life's Promise

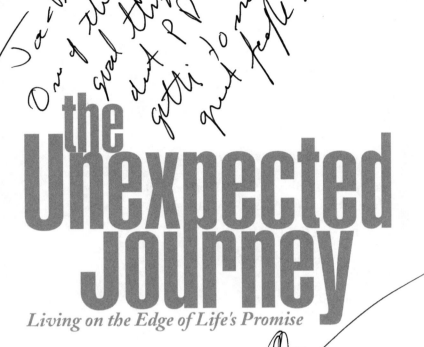

Joe-Deb,
One of the few
great things
about PD's is
gettin to meet
great people.

the Unexpected Journey

Living on the Edge of Life's Promise

by

George L. Johnston

AMBASSADOR INTERNATIONAL
GREENVILLE, SOUTH CAROLINA & BELFAST, NORTHERN IRELAND

www.ambassador-international.com

The Unexpected Journey

Living on the Edge of Life's Promise

*Library of Congress Cataloging-in-Publication Data
available from the publisher.*

Printed in the United States of America

Paperback ISBN: 978-1-935507-26-0
Hardback ISBN: 978-1-935507-27-7

Cover Design & Page Layout by David Siglin of A&E Media

AMBASSADOR INTERNATIONAL
Emerald House
427 Wade Hampton Blvd.
Greenville, SC 29609, USA
www.ambassador-international.com

AMBASSADOR BOOKS
The Mount
2 Woodstock Link
Belfast, BT6 8DD, Northern Ireland, UK
www.ambassador-international.com

The colophon is a trademark of Ambassador

This book is published in association with:
Paul Shepherd
SHEPHERD'S PUBLISHING SERVICES
www.shepherdps.com

Patti M. Hummel
President & Agent
THE BENCHMARK GROUP LLC, Nashville, TN
www.benchmarkgrouppublishers.com

This book was edited by:
Vicki Huffman, VP/Senior Editor
The Benchmark Group LLC, Nashville, TN
benchmarkgroup2@aol.com

This book is dedicated to the memory
of my maternal grandfather

George August Lider

TABLE OF CONTENTS

Preface   11

View from the Park Bench   17

Preparing for Liftoff   25

Don't Call Me ...   33

Do Numbers Matter?   41

Woof Woof   49

What to Lay Down – What to Pick Up   55

The Dog Who Ate Advent   63

You Were Awake When He Stuck a Wire *Where*?   71

Reflections Outside the Box   81

It's the *Qualia*, Stupid   89

Journey to the Dark Side   97

Origins: The Elusive Mystery   109

The Politics of Parkinson's   117

The Road Ahead   127

Acknowledgments   134

Bury your dead.
Comfort the mortally wounded.
Provide for the injured.
Don't envy the unscathed;
their day will come.
Break camp.

PREFACE

I am, in no particular order of priority: a Texan by birth and a Californian by choice; a Southern Baptist by birth and an Episcopalian by choice; a Christian by spiritual birth and choice; a Mayflower descendant by birth and an attorney by choice; and a father and grandfather by choice. I am steeped in the cultural characteristics or memes of Christianity. It is my spiritual underpinning—the descriptive metaphor for all that I am—and the lens by which I see all that is in the world. Because of it, I am comfortable with those who are likewise steeped in the peaceful memes of their birth, be they Islamic, Buddhist, Hindu, Scientific Rationalist or any number of other memes that are the birthrights of many in this world.

I am also (possibly by birth but not choice) one of 1 to 1.5 million people in the United States, and approximately 4 million people in the world, who has Parkinson's Disease, a currently incurable degenerative disorder of the brain. Parkinson's Disease

(PD) results in the accelerated death of the cells in the *Substantia Nigra* portion of the brain responsible for the production of the powerful neurotransmitter dopamine, the chemical primarily responsible for movement and movement-related functions in the human body. Furthermore, I am one of 100,000 to 150,000 people in the United States and approximately 400,000 people in the world diagnosed with Young Onset Parkinson's, characterized simply by being diagnosed before the age of 50. I was 43 in 1994 when I was diagnosed with PD.

The aphorisms[1] that you will find scattered throughout this book were a project that grew out of my morning walks in 2003-2004. That was a particularly depressing time. I had gone through a divorce which included a number of other losses: the loss of the affection of my children, the loss of my law practice, the loss of my ability to work at my chosen (or any other) profession or job and the loss of my financial resources. It was also the beginning of my recovery from eight years of compulsive gambling. At that time, the only hours that I could count on being physically and mentally functional at the same time were the two hours after I awoke in the morning, a phenomena that many with PD have in common. It is thought to be the result of the remaining brain cells stockpiling dopamine because they have "rested" during the night.

Every day without fail during this period I took long walks and tried to maintain focus on one particular aspect of life. By

---

1 Aphorisms, Haiku poetry, and short stories are great vehicles for those of us with limited energy and focus.

the end of a 7- or 8-mile walk, my ruminating would usually produce what I came to call a "Life Rule." Knowing that might sound a bit pedantic and authoritarian, I have since referred to them as lodestones, those naturally magnetic rocks *picked up* along my walk. In middle English, lodestone also meant "leading stone." And leading stones they are, having led me to bring into focus many aspects of life that remained unexamined prior to my diagnosis with PD.

The chapters in the book came about as the result of a commitment I made to my local Parkinson's Association, the Parkinson's Association of Northern California, to write a column for our monthly newsletter, "The Park Bench." These columns, called "Views from the Park Bench," were created with the belief that I had an ability to describe PD from the inside out, instead of the outside in: an insider's guide to the condition, so to speak. The response that I received from those with PD, their caretakers, and others who cared but were not exposed to the condition on a daily basis, convinced me there was a value in my insights beyond a local base. By intertwining those columns with the lodestone project, I hope that I am able to convey a sense of what it means to live at the edge of life's promise and bring hope to those who still struggle in the wilderness of the outsider. Whatever has marked those with PD for that role in this lifetime, I want to remind us that there are wonders yet to explore and value to the continued struggle.

You may wonder if this is a book about PD, helpful only to those whose lives have been touched by this disease. I hope not. Rather, it is intended to be about the human condition and is written for those who face a struggle in life greater than their ability to handle on their own. Those struggles bear many names, and include all chronic illnesses, addictions, the death of loved ones, loss of physical functionality, or numerous other of life's all too common tragedies. And they may be struggles fought for a week, a year or a lifetime. But they are common to all of us in that they focus our attention on our mortality, limitations and shortcomings. In the end, the types of struggles that I am referring to are those that lead to one of two conclusions: either we accept dependency on those around us for love, support and encouragement, or we accept despair and death. There really aren't any other choices.

Accepting dependency on other members of society brings the realization that that resource would not be there unless there was in others a dependency on something greater than the sum of the parts; that there must be a dependency on some transcendent bond that holds and focuses us together as a people. And out of this dependency comes a realization of what love is and what it can be. We also come to realize that dependency is not a negative word or concept, but is at the heart of the human struggle for meaning. For all of us are dependent on one another, for love, strength, compassion, hope, joy and purpose. It is in that mutual dependency that we find all of our companions for this lifetime, our true soul mates, and in that journey we find our dependency on God.

I hope that all who walk a little of my "Unexpected Journey" with me can come away with a sense of the power of the elemental strengths and mysteries along this road. I believe that understanding can help them find their source of love, strength and hope for the battles yet to come.

The whole image of the still pond and the single pebble is false. We all arrive at life with billions having come before and there will be billions coming after, all of varying sizes and trajectories. We each make our individual ripple and it counts, but it is impossible to ever predict its impact, course or effect.

Chapter 1

VIEW FROM THE PARK BENCH

I grew up on what Coronado and the Conquistadors called the Staked Plains. The white settlers when they came in the 19th century affectionately called these plains the Old Baldys. Modern cartographers call the area either the Panhandle of Texas or the High Plains. I apologize to the Comanche for not knowing what they called it, although I am sure it was a sacred word in their tongue. I called it *home*.

I grew up a privileged white male in the 1950s who dreamed of becoming an astronaut, an outfielder for the Yankees, the Lone Ranger, or Dave Guard of the Kingston Trio. Or all of them at once, if possible. The town I grew up in, Amarillo, means yellow in Spanish. I thought it meant "Look north, south, east or west 100 miles, and you won't see a hill higher that one foot above your bootlaces." But the vistas were grand. Being able to see those horizons stretching off so far in the distance made me imagine that my life would be similarly unlimited. Nothing to stop me, nothing to slow me down. Get on that road and you can drive forever. I understood the promise of Route 66.

Nurtured on Ray Bradbury, Arthur C. Clark, Robert Heinlein, Edgar Rice Burroughs, Ayn Rand and the Bible, I figured any obstacle that I would meet in life was surmountable. Surely I could dream myself out of it, science myself out of it, man myself out of it, money myself out of it or—if all else failed—let God pull me out of it. Wrong, wrong, wrong, and wrong. (Not necessarily wrong on the God issue, but it didn't work the way I expected.) Nevertheless, I survived falling off cliffs in Palo Duro Canyon, getting stuck in the open in a tornado/hail storm that should have killed everyone in the car, keeping my strike-anywhere matches and my Black Cat firecrackers in the same pocket of my jeans, running through plate-glass windows, and numerous other things that no Federal Child Safety Program had yet been developed to protect me from. Obviously, I assured myself, if these things didn't kill me, nothing could. I was made of sterner stuff.

...those horizons stretching off so far in the distance made me imagine that my life would be similarly unlimited. Nothing to stop me, nothing to slow me down.

I played baseball as both a pitcher and the home run leader on my team. So it occurred to me (albeit to no one else) that I was probably a nascent Babe Ruth. I ran the quarter-mile in high school track, was the drum major for my high school band, and sang the lead in our high school musical. (All right, if you must know, it was *Lil' Abner*.)

An all-round American boy, full of dreams, directions and desires.

Nobody was kind enough to warn me that lurking somewhere on my DNA strand was a combination of genetic markers that would create a weakness that by the time I was 43 would manifest itself in a diagnosis of Parkinson's Disease. All the promises and strength of youth, all the college and professional degrees, all the well-laid plans that required a strong hand and unlimited energy, all the sacrifices my family made to boost me to a place where I could manifest the destiny seemingly imprinted in me as a child, vanished in September 1994. That was when I was told that all the tests to rule out something else were negative. What was left was PD.

> I remember asking him what I could do about it. His answer: "Nothing."

I remember the doctor. I remember his office. I remember the brochures on Parkinson's Disease I looked at in his waiting room. I remember asking him what I could do about it. His answer: "Nothing."

I think that those of us who are diagnosed with PD or any other life-altering condition remember the circumstances in the same way that those who were alive when John Kennedy was assassinated remember that tragedy. This one was so much more personal though. Unforgettable!

My body had betrayed me and I took it personally. I would observe my tremors as if looking at a foreigner, an outcast: someone or something that did not belong. As a youth growing up in church I had heard the term "leper" used many times to describe those who were physically or ritually unclean or outcast. Now I knew what it felt like to be categorized as such, even if only by myself.

It is 15 years later now, and my view from the "Park Bench" has gone through many changes during that time. From denial, to hope, to despair, to apathy and back again. I have sat here and seen and experienced them all. I have at least reached a point in my travels with PD that I no longer walk the road alone but am now accompanied by those who share the same burdens either personally or vicariously—friends, colleagues and companions.

From denial, to hope, to despair, to apathy and back again.

This book includes some of my thoughts and observations about my journey with PD—my time on the Park Bench. Come on by, sit a while and enjoy the view. You are welcome here.

LODESTONES

If your doctor tells you that 99% of all people diagnosed with your condition die within 6 months, spend ALL your time studying the other 1%.

Regardless of the strength of the enemy, it is better to go into battle with 100 men who say "We can" than with 1,000 who say "We aren't sure."

Figure out what your birthright is. Don't sell it.

Friends are like teeth. Once lost, they can never be adequately replaced. Brush and floss daily.

LODESTONES

For good mental health, walk against the traffic at least one time each day.

If you haven't read the Book of Proverbs recently, do it. Then evaluate those you have elected to govern your public life and those that you allow to manage your economic life by its principals. If they don't measure up, REPLACE THEM.

It is better to struggle happily than to succeed miserably.

There are not two sides to every story.
There are usually at least ten.

LODESTONES

Find out what "Walk in Beauty" means. Do it.

Meditate on the following passage from Boris
Pasternak's Dr. Zhivago at least once a month: "One
day Laura went out and did not come back.... She
died or vanished somewhere, forgotten as a nameless
number on a list which was afterwards mislaid."
Vow never to let this happen to a friend or loved one.

Chapter 2

Preparing for Liftoff

[Johnnie]	*"I was so tired today …"*
[Audience]	*"How tired were you?"*
[Johnnie]	*"I was so tired that …"*

How can I possibly describe to someone without PD what it means when I say that I am tired, out of energy, kaput in the put-put, no goose in the caboose? How do I tell my spouse, son and/or daughter, grandchild, friend, etc., that it doesn't matter how much the tickets cost? That it doesn't matter if Ernie and Doris are only going to be here one more day and unless we see them tonight it may be years before we get another chance. That it doesn't matter our granddaughter only graduates from grade school once and she will be so disappointed if grandpa isn't in the audience beaming (people with PD don't beam, but you know what I mean). That it doesn't matter if fire is spreading from the kitchen into the front hallway, I just am too completely drained to get up off the couch and get out the door. That it ... well, you get the point.

> It doesn't matter if fire is spreading from the kitchen into the front hallway, I just am too completely drained to get up off the couch and get out the door.

I find that I spend much of my time trying to come up with ways to explain to family and friends what it feels like to be trapped in this body. Trying to explain to disappointed eyes that I can love you but still not be able to go with you for a simple walk around the block and that my being stuck in this recliner is not a matter of choice. The explaining itself can become an exhausting exercise. But it is one that must be undertaken if people without PD are going to be able to not take personally behavior from their loved one with PD. Behavior that is too often viewed or labeled as indifference, sloth, anger, and withholding of love or affection, just to name a few.

My best analogy so far comes from the time when I was actively flying as a private pilot. Think of the person with PD as an aviation pilot, the person without PD as an automobile driver. (The fuel for either will equate to dopamine released by the brain.) For the private pilot, calculating on-board aviation fuel requirements for your planned trip is the most important calculation you make before rolling out on the tarmac. Although the most important, it is only one of a myriad of things the private pilot must consider before lifting off.

For those driving automobiles, gas is not an overriding concern as they pull out of their driveways. The one driving an automobile also doesn't give much thought to precipitation, heat or cold, cloudy or clear skies, wind, total weight of all passengers, luggage and other paraphernalia stowed in the trunk, proper inflation of tires, and the availability of a restroom after departure. While these things can affect the nature of the trip and the comfort of all passengers, none of them, singly or together, can put the lives of passengers at risk if trouble is discovered with any of them after the trip has started. Why? Simple. Gas stations are plentiful.   Even in the worst-case scenario of running out of gas, you can park your car on the side of the road and hitch a ride to the next station. Rest stations are provided at reasonable intervals and, for a weather-related reason, you can pull over and wait out the storm in relative comfort.

Each morning the "little man in my head" must calculate how much dopamine this body is going to need to make it through the tasks of the day.

Pilots in command of an aircraft cannot be that casual when it comes to fuel. The aircraft pilot does not have the luxury of flexibility; he has to be precise about all matters that affect the ability of the aircraft to reach its intended destination. Weight, wind, weather, all affect how long and how far the plane can go between "gas stations." And trust me, if you run out before you get to one, you can't pull over and hitch a ride to get a gallon. All anticipated events and parameters that govern the use of fuel must be considered.

Similarly, each morning the "little man in my head" must calculate how much dopamine this body is going to need to make it through the tasks of the day. He also must determine just how many tasks will make it to the list. Many variables are in the mix he considers:

» Temperature. The internal thermometer of people with PD is out of sync; warm to the non-PD person is HOT to me.

» Weight: each extra pound of weight that my body carries is an additional burden on my dopamine reserves.

» Weather: inclement weather may inhibit the speed of someone without PD; it SLOWS ME DOWN.

» Distance to be traveled: getting there is one thing, but can I make it back? Round trips are tricky.

» What unanticipated problems may arise? Problems to someone with PD mean STRESS and STRESS means burning extra dopamine.

When I run out of fuel, I drop like a stone, just like an airplane, the only difference being that I can't glide for even a few moments. Add to this the overwhelming feeling of fatigue that overcomes me. If you know how heavy the "lead" blanket they put over you when you get an x-ray is, imagine clothes of a similar weight suddenly being placed on your body. (That is what it feels like to me.)

And it hurts.

The fatigue hurts in a way that I have never been able to adequately describe. It is not a sharp, slicing pain or a dull, aching pain; nor is it the throbbing pain of a headache. It is a body ache that demands one thing and one thing only. My body must stop whatever it is doing. Not "buck up" and fight through another 30 minutes. Not 10 minutes. Not 1 minute. NOW, STOP whatever it is that is sucking the last fume of fuel out of my tank. Make the hurt go away. Make the unbearable heaviness of being (my apologies to Milan Kundera) go away.

Now to the bright side (you were hoping there was one, weren't you?). I can refuel. I can fly again. I can feel again. But it ain't gonna be quick, folks. It takes time for the levedopa to kick in, the few remaining active cells in my brain still producing dopamine

> When I run out of fuel, I drop like a stone, just like an airplane, the only difference being that I can't glide for even a few moments.

to start pumping, my body to recover for the next journey. So, come sit on the Park Bench with me while I recover. Come hold some of the sweetness of life with me in shaky hands.

Like Icarus, those of us with PD fly too close to the sun each time we take flight. We push the edge of the envelope whenever we can, even though the envelope gets smaller each year. We drink deeply of what life has to offer whenever we can lift the cup. We haven't abandoned you, don't abandon us. We are still here, just quieter. We remember who we love and why.

We remember.

LODESTONES

Brevity takes time.

In the "rock, paper, scissors" game of the
soul, spirit always trumps matter.

Every battle is won at the last minute.

Be alert to opportunities for redemption.
Acquiesce gratefully.

Don't stone prophets.

The body is God's teaching tool.

LODESTONES

We all live on borrowed time. Your first query should be: who it is borrowed from? Your second query should be: what for?

Assume in every encounter with other human beings that your attitude toward them will set the tone for the rest of THEIR day.

Grief denied, or not fully exhausted, warps the soul and clouds the spirit. In its own time, it must be completely hammered out on life's anvil for clarity of vision to be restored.

When you are with a friend, don't keep track of time.

Chapter 3

WELL, YOU CAN CALL ME RAY, OR YOU CAN CALL ME JAY, BUT DON'T CALL ME ...

PARKIE. No, don't. Really. I'm not kidding. You can safely bury this word in the vocabulary dustbin of your mind and never let it see the light of day again.

I was sitting in a group discussing health care reform (haven't we all?) when someone looked at me and said, "And what does the *Parkie* contingent have to add to this debate."

Reflecting on that moment I was actually grateful, for the first time, that I was suffering from PD, because if I could have quickly gotten out of the chair I was sitting in, I would have raised my shaking fist and …

if I could have quickly gotten out of the chair I was sitting in, I would have raised my shaking fist and …

I am a 58-year-old man. I have my B.A. and J.D. I have been licensed to practice law in the State of California for 29 years. I sat for and passed the New York Bar exam at 46 years old just to see how I would do compared to a room full of 25 year olds. I am admitted to, and have practiced in, the Federal Courts for the Eastern and Northern Districts of California and the Western District of Michigan, have conducted litigation *Pro Hac Vice* in the Federal Courts in Puerto Rico (remind me never to sue Bacardi in Puerto Rico again), have litigated for many years major commercial and corporate litigation in the trial courts at 60 Centre Street in mid-town Manhattan, have conducted over 200 depositions throughout the United States and Canada and, for about five years in the mid-90s, lived one week per month in the corporate apartment in New York while taking care of business on the east coast. All that to say: if anybody back then had called me a *Parkie* or the diminutive of any appellation, I would have kindly and gently (but verbally) ripped his face off. And I did half the 90's under a diagnosis of idiopathic Parkinson's Disease.

So what happened? What has changed about me (and what has changed about you, too?) that allows people to feel comfortable describing you or me by any diminutive description? How can any of us, regardless of age, who deals with PD or any other life-changing condition be addressed so as to both recognize our past and acknowledge our present? How can we be addressed as persons who are infinitely more than the condition we carry in our bodies?

Well, for me "George" would be nice. Or even: "How do the lawyers (firefighters, schoolteachers, police officers, insurance professionals, etc.) in the room feel about …?" If you are going to ask my opinion as a part of a group, ask about that group that brought strength and adult responsibilities to my life, not the group that sends signals to everyone else that I may be weak or incapable of playing a full-contact sport. I may not be up to leading the charge up San Juan (or Bunker, or Pork Chop) Hill, but I have led charges like it before, and I can certainly be included in the planning and execution stages for one now.

> How can we be addressed as persons who are infinitely more than the condition we carry in our bodies?

Don't get me wrong. Cassius Clay I am not. But a wily and seasoned Mohammad Ali I am. I can't multi-task anymore, but I can mono-task and can do it quite well, thank you. I cannot write epic poetry, but I am pretty good at writing Haiku.

All of us have life stories to tell, myriad moments of triumph and tragedy. Times we figuratively "ran with the bulls" (some even literally), dragged a fellow firefighter from a burning house, closed the biggest deal ever to be brought into the office, caught the biggest fish seen in the river for a decade, spoke truth to power and lived to tell about it, and in one way or another made a difference in this world of ours. We don't want to be sidelined by being referred to in a manner meant to point out and highlight our weaknesses. Nor do we want to be described in terms more appropriate to a group of cute, helpless but lovable children.

For those of you reading this who have PD, don't allow yourself to be so quickly marginalized. Fight, with every bit of dopamine you can squeeze out of those last remaining cells, to be recognized for your strengths. Don't try to do five things at once: pick the one thing that you can do with the time you have. And do it WELL. Don't ask to be excused for your weaknesses, but ask to be included because of your strengths.

No one thinks twice if a clown is a little slow or stumbles around a bit. That is simply what clowns do. Gene used the weaknesses of PD to make Mr. Bumbles a wonderful clown.

You will be amazed at what may emerge.

A man named Gene Luttrell personified this for me. I swear that man must have wrestled bears when he was young. Sometimes I caught myself thinking that the only reason anyone ever noticed signs of PD in Gene was because he was trying to make you feel comfortable and not alone. Kind of like sending a secret signal that "It's O.K. I have to deal with it, too. You can get through this."

I believe that one of the ways Gene chose to exhibit his strength was through becoming a clown. "Mr. Bumbles" was able to mask some of the outward manifestations of PD by incorporating that into his clown persona. No one thinks twice if a clown is a little slow or stumbles around a bit. That is simply what clowns do. Gene used the weaknesses of PD to make Mr. Bumbles a wonderful clown. I loved that man.

Never in the farthest reach of my imagination would I ever have considered calling Gene a "Parkie." I always thought of Gene in terms of "Sir" or "Mr. Luttrell" or "Hey, Mr. Bumbles." I can only hope that I learn to live my life in such a deep and meaningful way that I can engender that same type of respect one of these days.

LODESTONES

Family can never be lost, they can only be misplaced.
(Now where did we put Aunt Edna?)

Given the price you have to pay for it, relative to other
things you can ask God for in this lifetime, wisdom is
highly overrated.

The test of one's respect for their God is not whether
or not they kneel to pray at church, synagogue or
mosque, but whether or not they kneel to pray when
they are at home alone.

Lodestones

Lawyers are simply a manifestation of peoples' unwillingness to solve their problems among themselves in a civil manner. Therefore: be alert to your impact on your neighbors. Be respectful to your spouse and children. Be fair with your weights and measures. Be cautious with what you unleash in your community (whether it be a dog, a product or an idea). Be generous with your talents. Tend your own garden. Fear your God. Practice these rules and lawyers will disappear within one generation.

There is one great Truth.

LODESTONES

The inner spirit of all gifts from parents to their children
should focus on providing wings, not anchors.

Without loyalty, there is no tragedy.
Without tragedy, there is no love.

Telling the truth never lost anyone a true friend.

Let go and allow yourself to be swept up in the great
ocean of life. Let your spirit free also;
it will act as your buoy.

Chapter 4

DO NUMBERS MATTER?

I was thinking while listening to competing news networks trying to decide how many people showed up for a protest event in Washington, D.C., how obsessed we have all become with numbers. The most conservative estimate was 70,000. The most liberal estimate was 1 to 1.5 million.

Now come on folks, haven't we reached a point with our advanced technology and satellite cameras that can read a license plate number off a car from low-earth orbit that we can do better than this? Politics aside, this is a HUGE discrepancy, one that our age of accurate measurement and scientific precision cannot tolerate, right?

That started me thinking about the figures I heard 16 years ago when I was first diagnosed with PD. At that time, in 1994, the estimates in the literature and available on the internet indicated that there were 1.5 to 2 million people diagnosed with PD in the United States, 10-15% of this number were considered "young onset" (diagnosed before age 40, although that designation later changed to before age 50), and there were 50,000 new cases diagnosed each year.

Over the last five years I have read differing opinions in the literature as to what were the correct figures, most accepting the 1.5-2 million figures as being accurate. Recently I read in a National Parkinson Foundation (NPF) brochure that there are 1 million people with PD in the United States, 10-15% of this number considered to be "young onset" (diagnosed before age 50), and there are 50,000 new cases diagnosed each year.

My first thought when seeing these new figures was: what happened to the extra 500,000 to 1,000,000 people counted to have been diagnosed with PD in 1994? My second thought was what did we do with the 750,000 newly diagnosed people from 1994 to 2009 (i.e. 50,000 new cases per year)? My third thought was that since the defined age of young onset changed from 40 to 50, why did the percentage of young onset in the total population not change?

(Estimates) indicated that there were 1.5 to 2 million people diagnosed with PD in the United States,…and there were 50,000 new cases diagnosed each year.

Either we have had an unreported epidemic of unprecedented proportion that killed off 50% or more of the people in the US with PD, or we have a serious problem accounting for ourselves. (It makes one look at the question "Am I my brother's keeper?" in a new light.)

One of the first questions that may spring to your mind is "So what?" Even if there are "only" one million people with PD, that is still nothing to sneeze at. It's a substantial number of people that need attention. But on further thought, in this day and age of unprecedented concern over health cost, universal health care, health care delivery by the private sector vs. public sector, rationing of health care products and procedures, etc., isn't it incumbent on those of us that deal with PD to come up with figures that can be relied upon? We may not know the "why" of us, or the "how" of us, but can't we at least know the "how many" of us?

Yes, I know there are issues of privacy that prevent gathering accurate records from doctors and that the numbers for idiopathic PD may be exacerbated by PD +, or those cases that are diagnosed as PD but turn out not to be PD, or myriad other reasons that could be paraded forth to excuse not having a more accurate accounting of all of us. But something tells me that someone, somewhere, has a handle on either a better count or at least a better way to count.

> Isn't it incumbent on those of us that deal with PD to come up with figures that can be relied upon? We may not know the "why" of us, or the "how" of us, but can't we at least know the "how many" of us?

You can't tell me that there isn't someone sitting around at the Sinnemet[2] factory looking for ways to accurately estimate this year's production figures by counting the number of people that they think need their product. (I know they have someone at the Jelly Belly factory!) And the same counting is going on at the other pharmaceutical companies that manufacture the other drugs that are only or primarily used for PD. Remember, these guys are still in it for profit, and overproduction means less money to go around at the top. (We all know that it doesn't go around at the bottom.)

Now to answer your "so what?" query, let's look at one of the practical reasons that this matters for those of us in the trenches fighting PD (or living with PD or both) on a daily basis. When I go to the capitol, either in Sacramento or Washington D.C., to lobby my representative for legislation that benefits those living with PD, what is the first thing my representative wants to know and know accurately? Simple. HOW MANY OF HIS/HER CONSTITUANTS HAVE PD? On a national level, 2,000,000 potential voters means more than 1,000,000 potential voters. And if I can assure my representative that these are not made-up numbers but can give them chapter and verse that lends authenticity and accuracy to my representations, then I have an audience that is listening.

I am reminded of the parable in the New Testament where the shepherd leaves his flock of 99 sheep to go look for the one that is lost.

2 **Primary drug of choice for treatment of symptomatic aspects of Parkinson's.**

If I am lobbying on a city, county, state or national level for money or benefits to flow to my group, the size and accuracy of the group I am lobbying for couldn't be more important. If there are really 2,000,000 of us out there, but the person with the purse strings thinks there are only 1,000,000, and they set their budget for funding on the lower number … you get the picture.

On a more personal level, I am reminded of the parable in the New Testament where the shepherd leaves his flock of 99 sheep to go look for the one that is lost. I wonder if we are too fast and loose with our counting, if we are paying too much attention to the whole flock but not enough attention to the one who may have gone astray.

In short, one of our friends with PD that is unaccounted for is one too many.

LODESTONES

Your body doesn't need to be convinced by Madison Avenue that it needs water.

Exercise, if for no other reason than so that you can eat real butter.

Every encounter with another human being is an act of ministry, both to their soul and to yours. Make it a ministry of humility and strength; they are not incompatible.

There are no rules at Christmas, only love, which by its nature transcends all rules. That is the true miracle of the season.

Take life seriously, not yourself.

LODESTONES

If we took all the time we spent resolving and applied it to becoming, we would be there by now.

Share joy, as it dies if hoarded. It is the yeast of life.

Actions that we think carry the most significance in our lives often do not. Those that we think carry no significance sometimes turn out to have the greatest. Each action, therefore, requires equivalent attention and care as to consequences.

If you are feeling emotionally and spiritually "let down" after Christmas, maybe it is because the primary Gift of the season was left unopened beneath the tree.

Chapter 5

WOOF WOOF

Akua, my service dog, had been after me to let him write a Park Bench column ever since I started. I kept telling him that it was not as simple as he thought and that it took a lot of time, patience and vocabulary. But due to my inability to get one column done on time, he had to "Cowdog Up." Granted his debut in the publishing world wasn't very lengthy, but he held the space open for me, which is sometimes all we can ask of a good service dog. Actually, I think he put it together quite well. I was especially impressed with his getting "neuro-stimulator" in there!

Barks from the park bench

"George had his neuro-stimulator battery changed this month. While he is doing fine, there were some programming functions that were not quite right and, although they are straightened out now, it has really limited his ability to meet a deadline. He asked me to write his column for him, but my human vocabulary just isn't large enough yet to fill up all this space. George will be back on the bench for next month's issue."

Woof Woof – Akua

(To expand Akua's explanation a little: the surgery went well and was uneventful, except that the magnets in the neuro-stimulator device had some adjustment problems. Over the course of the next week my unit recycled every time I was too close to a strong magnet. By the end of the week, I was stuck on permanent recycle and had to journey back to UC San Francisco Medical Center for a complete review of the parameters on the transmitter which resulted in a fix of the problem. It was an instructive week overall as it reminded me of the chancy nature of life in general and of living with Parkinson's in particular.)

His debut in the publishing world wasn't very lengthy, but he held the space open for me, which is sometimes all we can ask of a good service dog.

LODESTONES

An acquaintance will slow his/her pace
to yours when you walk.
An acquaintance will strive to increase his/her pace
to yours when you walk.
A friendship is formed when acquaintances meet,
confer and compromise.

At least once a month invite friends and family over to
make bread from scratch. Bake and enjoy while warm.

In making resource-use decisions, bear in mind that
you don't want the title of the book chronicling your
generation's stewardship of the planet to be, "Eating
the Earth: An Addict's Guide."

LODESTONES

If ten percent (10%) or more of what you pay for fast food is channeled by the manufacturer through Madison Avenue to convince you that your body needs it, it doesn't.

Strength, whenever requested, will always be provided for righteous acts.

Strength, when it comes, often wears an unfamiliar face. Anticipate unexpected appearances.

LODESTONES

Faith is hammered out on a harsh anvil.

The laws of probability are not sequential; the counter is reset at every coin toss. What distinguishes human beings from coins is belief and will. Hence the statistical skew in the direction of failure for pessimists and success for optimists.

Strive to distinguish between subjective needs and objective necessities.

Chapter 6

What to Lay Down – What to Pick Up

I had been contemplating topics for an upcoming column ranging from the practical to the esoteric. I considered writing

about service dogs for people with PD until my mind drifted to the philosophical debate in the literature about consciousness of the meaning of the word "qualia" when it comes to a description of our interaction with the world and other people. (See Chapter 10 where I did write

Maps just describe [it] as "dangerous one-lane unpaved road, do not travel." For once I can attest that a map did not overestimate what was in store ahead.

about the qualia.) But when standing at the summit of Haleakela on Maui—which would be the highest mountain in the world at 30,000 feet if only they could include the 20,000 feet underwater—another subject forced its way into my consciousness. It arrived there as a result of a drive my fiancée Darlene and I had taken the day before.

For those of you who have been to Maui or for those who have travelled there in your minds, you may have encountered the fabled "Highway to Hana." This is a portion of highway (and I do mean a portion as it could not be counted a whole highway in anyone's definition) that winds its way precariously around the northeastern portion of the island though countless turns and tumbles. It is a ride definitely not for the weak of stomach or faint of heart.

My real epiphany did not come on the way to Hana though; it came on another stretch of road on the northwestern portion of the island that the maps just describe as "dangerous one-lane unpaved road, do not travel." For once I can attest that a map did not overestimate what was in store ahead. But I was not one to pass up a challenge. I felt secure in the knowledge that the Jeep that we had rented from Dollar could work miracles on any island terrain. And I, as a bionic Parkinsonian, was surely up to any challenge, so we chose to set forth into the unknown.

I say "we" but it was really I who chose as Darlene is not this stupid—there may be a more clever word, but stupid is as stupid does and it fits.

What we encountered was the textbook definition of "narrow one-lane road" except that it was in reality a 3⁄4-lane road at best. And, just to throw some spice into the mix, the road went through elevation changes like Akua goes through dog biscuits. We are not talking about up and down 100- or 200-feet inclines, we are talking up and down valleys that after all the hairpin switchbacks took you down 1,000 feet and back up in the space of one mile.

There is a legend on Maui about the little people that once inhabited the island and came out at night to build the low-lying rock fences that dot the island. Well, the inglorious imps must have built this road, too. At the deepest point of one of the gorges that we drove through we came upon a little village. I am convinced that the reason that this village exists is that the people who live there simply decided that living at the bottom of the gorge was better than being dashed to death in the fall from the cliffs. They live off the land and can salvage provisions from the ones that keep going up the other side and falling off.

> The road went through elevation changes like Akua goes through dog biscuits....up and down valleys that after all the hairpin switchbacks took you down 1,000 feet and back up in the space of one mile.

I know that some of you by this time think I am exaggerating, but if we had stopped the car on this road at most points, Darlene could not have opened the passenger side door because of the cliff face on her side. And if I had opened the driver's side door and stepped out, I would have fallen off the side of the cliff. At one point I began to wonder why I hadn't run into anyone coming the other way, when it occurred to me that the road was over quota for the day of the number of idiots allowed to drive it.

Then, out of nowhere, at the top of one of the gorges rising above the clouds, came a glorious flat plateau, shining in the sun. On it was a lovely two-story Victorian house with parking spaces for at least five cars. Low and behold, it was an art gallery. This begged several questions, such as what maniac architect, what maniac general contractor, what maniac property owner, what maniac landscape designer, what maniac artist, etc., would choose to build on such a location? Particularly in light of the fact that this was not the end of the one-lane road, which would have made some perverted sort of sense, but instead was simply a break halfway through the 15-mile drive from Hades.

The two women who were on duty at the gallery, with deep sunken eyeballs, sallow cheeks and pointed teeth, informed me that the owner of the gallery had lived there for 16 years and that her husband drove to town every day for supplies. (*Flies to town each night as a bat and sleeps each day in the crypt at the back of the gallery is more like it*, I thought.)

Having taken advantage of this brief reprieve, we realized that as much as we did not want to get back on this road to complete our journey, neither did we want to spend the rest of our lives at the "Bates Hotel and Art Gallery." We put the

Jeep in first gear and crept back on the highway, screaming at the top of our lungs: "I love you, I love you, I don't want to die today and not let you know."

Obviously, we made it back. If you don't think this story has a tie to the problems of living with Parkinson's, you are dead wrong. Living with Parkinson's for me is a daily struggle of ego with reality. My ego says I am still that young, vibrant, I-can meet-any-challenge man that I was when I was 30. Reality says that I am a 58-year-old man with Parkinson's Disease, who has had brain surgery to have metal rods implanted in my brain to alleviate most of the motor problems that I had to deal with pre-surgery, who still needs to take medication in order to have my body move at all, and who less than two months ago had a new neurotransmitter implanted in my chest that for ten days after the surgery gave me fits and left me totally at its magnetic whim. I say I want to be a responsible adult. Well, responsible adults don't do what I did that day; they don't put the lives of the people they love at risk for the sake of an adolescent fantasy that they are the next Indiana Jones.

> [It] is a daily struggle of ego with reality. My ego says I am still that young, vibrant, I-can meet-any-challenge man that I was when I was 30. Reality says that I am a 58-year-old man with Parkinson's Disease.

I have limitations. There are things in life that I can never do again (or could never do the first time). But this is O.K. This is life. This is my life. That life, if seen in the right perspective, is just as challenging, if not more so, mentally and physically as navigating that road in Maui. My adolescent ego needs just don't compare with the damage they can create—and for such limited rewards.

I have limitations. There are things in life that I can never do again (or could never do the first time). But this is O.K. This is life.

Maybe it is time to lay this down and pick up the life that I have. It might even be time to start looking into the wonders of calligraphy.

LODESTONES

If you neglect your faith, you will wake up one morning
to find that you have been working without a net.

Maybe there isn't a better mousetrap.

All one can do is leave the door open
and set a place at the table ...

Rocks are polished in a tumbler.

In life's race, no one sprints across the finish line.

Anomalies are the branches which fuel the spirit's fire.

LODESTONES

Measure a religion's efficacy by whether or not its epiphanies ultimately lead to engagement with, or withdrawal from, the world.

When preparing to face the world each day, don't just look at yourself in the mirror. Look deeper.

The superstructure can change with fashion and the seasons. The house will endure as long as its foundation is secure.

We own nothing in this life.
Everything is on long-term lease.

Chapter 7

THE DOG WHO
ATE ADVENT

During several periods of my life I was in Jungian therapy, a type of therapy that focuses a great deal on dream analysis. While I haven't formally participated in therapy for many years, the habits I acquired, particularly as regards writing down memorable or significant dreams, have remained.

In particular, my dream notebook records a dream I had in June 2006:

> *Had a great dream this morning about being out on a horse ranch with some people from my past. While I was there, I met an old Native American that lived in a hole in the ground with a little Queensland pup that he was protecting from the rest of the litter because he was gentler than the rest and had a special*

"spiritual" quality about him. When the pup tried to get out of the hole, the old man clung tightly to him and would not release him. Only when I went over and spoke to him and explained my love of the pup and his personality would he finally let me take him out of the "whole" and place him above ground. He made me feel like a good person, just being with such a fine animal and always brought a smile to my face as he went with me everywhere I went. He gave me a sense of belonging back with a tribe or group that I hadn't had for a long time.

Some dreams you can ignore, but this one I couldn't. I just happened to have a friend who bred Australian Cattle Dogs (Queensland Heelers). I told her the next time one of her dogs had a litter to let me know. The next spring, on March 13, she called to tell me that a new litter had just been born. Eight weeks later, I brought Akua home. (Akua means "ghost" or "spirit" in Hawaiian.)

Since then Akua has become my service dog in more ways than I can possibly recount. He is my constant companion. He is a steady pull hiking in the mountains when the hill is a bit too steep. He runs interference for me in crowds. (He was great at the De Young Museum in San Francisco when the Tut exhibit was there.) When I freeze, he is what gets me moving. When I am stuck on the couch, he pulls me up. When I become too self-absorbed with

> Akua has become my service dog in more ways than I can possibly recount. … He is my friend through good or bad, thick or thin, in rain or shine.

my PD, he reminds me that he has to have a walk, some food or water, a treat or just some attention. He is my friend through good or bad, thick or thin, in rain or shine.

Where I go, Akua goes: board meetings, restaurants, museums, art galleries, shopping, vestry meetings, hikes in the mountains, on the train to San Francisco (he particularly liked meeting my neurological team at UC San Francisco), grocery shopping, running on the beach ... you name it. If I am there, Akua is with me. Any questions as to whether or not he can be allowed in these places is quickly answered by a reference to the definition of service dog under the ADA (Americans with Disabilities Act).

The ADA defines a service animal as *"any* guide dog, signal dog, or other animal individually trained to provide assistance to an individual with a disability."* If animals meet this definition, they are considered service animals under the ADA, regardless of whether they have been licensed or certified by a state or local government. Service animals perform some of the functions and tasks that individuals with disabilities cannot perform for themselves. Guide dogs are one type of service animal, used by some individuals who are blind. This is the type of service animal with which most people are familiar. But there are service animals that assist persons with other kinds of disabilities in their day-to-day activities. The ADA cites examples of assistance including:

Alerting persons with hearing impairments to sounds.

Pulling wheelchairs or carrying and picking up things for persons with mobility impairments.

Assisting persons with mobility impairments with balance.

The ADA emphasizes that "a service animal is <u>not</u> a pet."

Akua didn't reach this point without training and socialization, but he didn't need to go through the same type of rigorous training that a service dog for the blind has to go through. (Although, there is no doubt in my mind that he could.) Most people with Parkinson's that I have discussed this with think this is the case, or they don't really think of the many ways that they could benefit from having a service animal.

Now, as to the title of this chapter. Although Akua is a wonderful service dog and the ADA declares that he is not a pet, he does have something in common with many pets: Akua loves to chew. Anything, anytime, anyplace. If I can't find my glasses, I check Akua's mouth. Same with my keys. So I shouldn't have been surprised when I couldn't find the brochure with Advent devotionals in it. It was usually kept on the breakfast table next to the Advent wreath. Sure enough, when I followed the "paper trail" (literally) there was Akua sitting in his bed, tail wagging, happily finishing off the pamphlet with a big smile on his face. Likewise, the next day I found the matchbook (usually next to the advent wreath) on his bed half-eaten. The candle is not missing yet, but any day now I expect him to burp up a candle, put his paws up on the table, and place it gently in the wreath.

After all, he is a service dog.

LODESTONES

In the beginning there was an infinitely small singularity, ... and the Word, ... and one truth. Then there was light. It was magnificent!

What does it say about us a nation that statistically the safest place to be to ensure that you will not be the subject of an Al Qaeda terrorist attack is inside a church?

When a leaf is ready to fall, it takes only the slightest breath from God to launch it on its journey.

Before you can run the good race, you had better acquire a pair of good shoes.

LODESTONES

Learn to distinguish in your heart the difference
between sorrow for the harm your actions have
caused yourself and sorrow for the harm your actions
have caused others. The first road leads to self-pity.
The second leads to the possibility of
reconciliation and redemption.

When you awake, embrace, like a child, the
mysterious sounds of the morning.

If we abandon the "faith of our fathers," we
shouldn't expect to inherit the riches which that
faith purchased.

LODESTONES

Christ is not understood in the United States today
because we don't understand or appreciate why
he didn't change teams when he was offered a
"better deal."

All diets rely on one thing for their success: discipline.
Therefore, it is not the diet but the attitude that results
in lost weight.

Chapter 8

YOU WERE AWAKE WHEN HE STUCK A WIRE WHERE?

Every one that I speak to who has PD shares a common perception that it is truly a "designer" disease, i.e., no two people have quite the same symptoms, take exactly the same medication, or have the same fluctuations of symptoms during the day. Similar, yes, but never the same.

That observation is borne out in my conversations with those with PD who are lucky enough to have had Deep Brain Stimulation surgery [DBS], which is the current state-of-the-art means of controlling the physical symptoms of the disease.

It is not a cure, but simply a means by which some, or most, depending on the individual, symptomatic manifestations of PD can be minimized without the use of medication. (In fact, a small minority of those who have DBS can go without medication, and almost all can reduce the amount that they took before the surgery.)

The procedure is "simple." They take what is essentially a Black and Decker drill, put two quarter-size holes in the top front of your skull, pull the plugs out, and then insert a whisper-thin titanium wire into one of three areas that control certain types of movement in your brain. Once they find the sweet spot, they replace the quarter-size circle of bone and secure it with some sort of cranial super glue, then run a wiring harness from the wires now in your brain down the side of your neck and terminate them in a neurotransmitter that is implanted in the upper part of your chest. The neurotransmitter is basically a souped-up Duracell (and no, you can't replace it at the watch department at Wal-Mart). All other things being equal, they then turn you on and "Bingo"—bionic brain, wired up and ready to go.

> They take what is essentially a Black and Decker drill, put two quarter-size holes in the top front of your skull, pull the plugs out, and then insert a whisper-thin titanium wire...

One of the great (?) things about this procedure is that you are awake all during the time that the wires are being implanted in your brain (about 4-5 hours if both sides are done in one surgery) in order that your surgeon can be sure that the wires are properly positioned. Your surgical team actually listens to the neurons in your brain communicating with each other. Finding the area where they are quiet and still is the goal. I think it must be similar to listening to whale songs. I will never forget looking my surgeon in the eye as he manipulated the wires in the language area of my brain and speaking, at his instructions, the days of the week as clearly as possible. "Monday, Tuesday, Wednesday, Urgualll, quiselbrot, hultivard, Sunday," etc. I completely lost my ability to speak the names of the days when the wire was moved just a millimeter into the wrong area. (Talk to me sometime about the concept of freedom of choice. One gets a whole new perspective on the entire concept after undergoing DBS.)

When the wires are finally set, the doctors put you completely to sleep (thank you, God), so they can install the wiring harness and the neurotransmitter.

In California, and perhaps in other states, there is a law that allows you to pin to your surgical gown anything that you want read aloud to you as you are being wheeled into the operating theatre. The day I was wheeled in, I had chosen Psalm 121 (NRSV) from the Old Testament:

"I lift up my eyes to the hills - from where will my help come?
My help comes from the LORD, who made heaven and earth.
He will not let your foot be moved; he who keeps you will not slumber.
He who keeps Israel will neither slumber nor sleep.
The LORD is your keeper; the LORD is your shade at your right hand.

The sun shall not strike you by day, nor the moon by night. The LORD will keep you from all evil; he will keep your life. The LORD will keep your going out and your coming in from this time on and forevermore."

Also by law in California you are allowed to request certain music be played during your surgery and to bring in your own CD. I started the party with The Beatles "Magical Mystery Tour." Go figure.

[You can] pin to your surgical gown anything that you want read aloud to you as you are being wheeled into the operating theatre...I had chosen Psalm 121.

My surgery was done on March 15, 2005. The ides of March. The day I was literally reborn, a reluctant phoenix rising from the ashes to face a new world.

The other date I will always remember in connection with my DBS surgery is December 8, 2004, the day I first met the surgical team at the University of California San Francisco Medical Center. That was the day that I would be evaluated for candidacy for the DBS procedure. (Only 15% of people with PD in the United States are qualified for DBS.)

While sitting in the waiting room, I engaged in the time-honored practice that we all participate in when in doctors' waiting rooms: finding the most recent issue of whatever magazine we can find that will help us pass the time. The magazine selection was sparse that day, and the only one that I could find to distract me was a September 2004 issue of *The New Yorker*. While flipping through it, I came across the following poem, which I proceeded to tear out of the magazine and subsequently have laminated to carry in my wallet. I read it every day, still. It reminds me every day that I am living on borrowed time and that there are more owed for my new life than I can ever repay.

"You who are lengthening your lives
with the best doctors and the best medicines
remember those who are shortening their lives
with the wars
that you in your long lives are not
preventing. ..."
by Yehuda Amichai, Translated from the Hebrew by Leon Wieseltier

My journey with PD is one that I never anticipated or could have imagined for myself. The truth is, all things being equal, if I had been born 50 years earlier, I would have been dead at this point in the progression of my PD. No adequate medications existed to calm the tremors or halt the steady progression of the condition. No adequate understanding existed to explain why what was happening to people who had these symptoms was happening, and essentially, once one reached the point of what I call terminal stillness (because stillness and complete lack of movement is truly the hallmark of the end stages of the disease), you were simply warehoused until you passed on. Yet here I was 11 years into my diagnosis, 54 years of age, having been "Rewired for Life," walking, hiking, working, off to lend my hands to the Red Cross in the wake of Katrina, experiencing the wonders of life once again. I began putting things on my calendar for the next year because I felt confident that my body would be able to go and I would be around to attend.

What was the worst side-effect from my DBS surgery? Research has indicated that the average weight gain 6 months after the surgery is 22 pounds. I gained every one of them. In doing so, I realized that the reason for the weight gain was simple: I no longer had the tremors or the dyskenisias connected with PD. I had essentially been running in place 24/7 for many years, but it had become background noise for me until it stopped. And trust me, I can live with that side effect.

And the best side effect? The stillness.

The STILLNESS!

I can't express to you the wonder and majesty of simply being still, voluntarily and normally. In the theatre watching a play, at a concert, watching TV, reading, in church, in court, driving, eating, lying in bed upon waking in the morning or when going to bed at night. The phrase from the Psalms, "Be still and know that I am God" took on a meaning to me that is difficult to express. These are the simplest of things, but so often we take them for granted.

Each day I mourn for those who for whatever reason are not able to have this procedure done or who have had the procedure done but have not obtained the same measure of benefits that I have. And knowing where I have been, I have the painful knowledge of where I am going. DBS is not a cure, and I know that every day the disease progresses. Every day I get closer to the way I was before, and the day will come when the electrical stimulation may not provide the same degree, or perhaps any degree, of symptomatic relief. We simply do not know. Remember "Flowers for Algernon" from literature classes in high school in the 1960's? I do.

This is when I take the Alfred E. Newman "What, Me Worry?" approach to life. In doing so, I remember a news report I heard about a New Yorker who had reached the age of 104. In his earlier years, he was billed as the "Strongest Man in the World" at Coney Island. He was out for a walk in Brooklyn, crossed the street and was run over by a truck. Unfortunately, he passed away that day at the hospital. And I'll bet you the last thing that gentleman had on his mind when he woke up that morning was that it was his day to die at 104—by being run over by a truck of all things! One thinks that if you live to that age, you have learned basic pedestrian/traffic rules.

Here I was 11 years into my diagnosis, 54 years of age, having been "Rewired for Life," walking, hiking, working, off to lend my hands to the Red Cross in the wake of Katrina, experiencing the wonders of life once again.

My time will end when it ends, and most likely in a manner totally unforeseen by me. It's best that I leave that to God and busy myself with all the joy that is waiting for me. And, hopefully when crossing the street, I'll always remember to look both ways.

LODESTONES

Save your money. With the exception of those with special medical needs, this is the only diet book you will ever need in this lifetime:
Chapter 1: Eat more calories than you burn, gain weight.
Chapter 2: Eat the same number of calories that you burn, maintain present weight.
Chapter 3: Eat less calories than you burn and lose weight.

In the end, all that wealth really provides is a more comfortable room to die in.

LODESTONES

At the heart of every perceived weakness or infirmity
is a strength waiting to be mined.

Leave nothing unsaid.

Every person's greatest fear is that one day they will
speak the deepest truth of their heart and no one will
be there to listen.

Try not to self-select yourself out of opportunities that
life presents, or goals that you would like to achieve.
We are rarely the best judges of our own talents and
abilities. Ergo, Woody Allen's observation that 95% of
success is simply showing up.

LODESTONES

On the ocean of life, members of your family are
both passengers and the boat.

Try to remember the wonder you felt as a child when
you first discovered the lesson of the prism: All
the colors of the universe emerge from a single,
undifferentiated beam of life.

We never see the light beam. We see only that
portion of the beam reflected back by life in its path.

He who dies with the most toys dies.
He who dies with no toys dies.
What is the real issue here?

Chapter 9

REFLECTIONS OUTSIDE THE BOX

It is amazing to me sometimes how I become so obsessed with my Parkinson's that anything outside that box has no meaning. Having lived with what many with Parkinson's affectionately call the "unwelcome stranger" for nigh on 16 years now, it has become so woven into every fabric and corner of my life that everything that I say or do seems to be colored with a PD background. I remember the interview that Michel J. Fox did with Barbara Walters in the late 90's. She asked him, "Is there ever any time during the day that you are not aware of the fact that you have Parkinson's?"

With only a brief moment for reflection, he replied simply, "No."

It takes something powerful to pull me out of my awareness of my PD, but such was the case on January 15, 2010, when Haiti was devastated by what I am sure will always be remembered by the people who live there as "*The* Earthquake." For a moment—actually more than a moment—I was transfixed by the horror and terror that were created in the lives of so many people. And for many moments my PD was not important, not even memorable. There simply are some things that happen in this life that so transcend our own problems, they make those problems that we cherish and polish each day lose their significance.

Catastrophes like the one that happened in Haiti have their lessons for those of us with lesser burdens to bear. Such a lesson was taught to me on August 29, 2005 when Hurricane Katrina hit New Orleans. Just six months earlier, on March 15, I had my DBS surgery. I was literally transformed from an invalid into a functioning, albeit still-struggling member of society. And seeing what was happening in New Orleans called out to me in the way no tragedy of any scope had touched me previously. Before you could whistle Dixie, I was at the Red Cross office in Sacramento finding out what I could do with my newly-found freedom from the symptomatic manifestations of PD. I knew what it was like to have lost it all, and the pictures and stories of those in New Orleans facing the same prospect galvanized my will.

> I was transfixed by the horror and terror that were created in the lives of so many people. And for many moments my PD was not important, not even memorable.

I endured several long arguments with representatives of the Red Cross, who said they weren't going to send someone that had just had brain surgery into a disaster zone. But my neurologist and neurosurgeon were willing to go to bat for me and say, "If he is willing to take the risk, he shouldn't be treated differently from any other volunteer." After drafting and signing a waiver holding the Red Cross harmless from anything that happened to me if I were deployed into the New Orleans area, three weeks after Katrina hit I was finally on my way to Louisiana with one of the first groups of Red Cross volunteers deployed from Sacramento to the disaster area.

I was assigned to a food kitchen in Belle Chase, Louisiana, about 10 miles south of downtown New Orleans, and for three weeks worked with the best group of individuals I have ever had the opportunity to know, putting out 3,000 hot meals a day for some of those who had lost everything overnight. I stood in line with 25-year-olds unloading water, food and other provisions from the back of 18-wheelers, and never broke a stride. Granted I took a nap every afternoon if I could, but others allowed me that. For those three weeks, I was so swept up in the tragedy of the lives of others that PD seemed a distant concern, not a daily companion. I will always treasure those times and equally treasure those

Three weeks after Katrina hit I was finally on my way to Louisiana with one of the first groups of Red Cross volunteers deployed from Sacramento to the disaster area.

doctors whose skill and concern gave me the opportunity to experience once again what it meant to be a fully-functional part of society.

One of the many lessons I learned from that trip was that having PD not only removes you from the joys of life, but the tragedies also. Feeling like and being a member of society require that you participate in its tragedies, as well as its triumphs. Feeling happy and feeling sad are likewise similar: they are both feelings and are equally missed by those of us with PD.

As I watched the news coverage of the earthquake relief efforts in Haiti, I revisited memories of my time working disaster relief in the wake of Katrina. I have had to remind myself that my PD has advanced these last 4 ½ years, regardless of the surgery, that I am 58, not 53, and that a country with little or no government control or involvement in the life of its population is not a place for any civilian non-disaster professional to be—with or without PD.

> Feeling like and being a member of society require that you participate in its tragedies, as well as its triumphs.

So I knew I had to sit this one out, contribute what I could financially, and hope that those stronger than myself would take this opportunity to involve themselves in assisting those in Haiti, both now and in the future. For just like Katrina in New Orleans, this situation will not be patched over or healed in a week, a month or a year. It will take decades for normalcy in any real sense to return to a region affected this way.

For those of us who must sit on the sidelines and watch disasters in any part of the world, we can also try to prepare ourselves in the event a similar emergency happens in our neighborhood, whether we live in flood zones or near earthquake fault lines. Perhaps the best thing we can do to prepare for an emergency is to lessen the impact of our limitations on those charged with taking care of the situation in our neck of the woods. How do we do that? At minimum:

[1] by making sure we have at least a one-month surplus supply of our medications in a watertight container in our homes, where it will be the first thing to grab in the event that an emergency arises;

[2] by keeping packed in a backpack that can be grabbed quickly enough loose-fitting and comfortable clothes for several days;

[3] by making sure that someone who doesn't live at our address has our list of medications, doctors and other pertinent medical information; and

[4] by making sure we are on file with Medic Alert and that we wear the medic alert bracelet or medallion at all times.

From my experience with Katrina, I can personally attest to the fact that emergency workers are relieved when they find people who have made these advance preparations. Just think for a moment what it would be like if you were alone in a disastrous situation, scared, running out of medication, without a change of clothes, and with no ability to communicate immediately to first responders pertinent medical information about your condition. It is not a pretty sight. So be prepared. That may be the best help those of us with debilitating neurological conditions will have to offer those who come to help us survive a disaster.

When you hear of the next disaster, pray especially for those who suffer from neurological disorders.

And pray. When you hear of the next disaster, pray especially for those who suffer from neurological disorders. Pray that they will be found by compassionate first responders who will be able to ascertain, understand and deal with their needs.

LODESTONES

Meditate on what life will be like if we become a country entirely of people who think like employees instead of patriots.

If outlining your autobiography does not cause you, on some level, to re-experience deep wells of sorrow and remorse, in addition to joy and thanksgiving, you are not ready to write it yet.

Whether we want to acknowledge it or not, we all draw our water from the same Well.

Better one rose well tended than a whole garden gone to seed.

LODESTONES

In real life, the race is not won by the proud, the strong
and the swift, for the track is not flat and straight.
Instead, it is won by the humble, the consistent and
the determined, as the path is crooked and rocky.

No one is disabled; everyone is limited. As with everything
else in life, it is simply a matter of degree and perspective.

Very few are selected as generals. Most of us simply
serve as the battlefield.

Always allow your grandchildren to reach deep into
your heart, where they can link the reality of your past
with the possibility of your future.

Chapter 10

It's the "Qualia", Stupid

In the early 70's, Jack Nicholson starred in a movie called *Five Easy Pieces*. It was a prodigal son story, and Nicholson played the character who had abandoned his family and promise as a young man to live a dissolute life below his talent and upbringing. Nicholson's character was a child prodigy on the piano and the fourth generation of classical musicians in his family. The story line centers around his fall and attempted redemption when he comes home to face his father, who has had a stroke and remains uncommunicative throughout the movie.

One of Nicholson's love interests corners him one day and insists that he play the piano for her. Reluctantly, he obliges and plays a series composed by Chopin called "Five Easy Pieces."

She focuses on his performance with rapt attention and, when he finishes, she heaps plaudits on him for his performance. She asks him how it feels to be able to produce such beautiful music. He responds, with the classic Nicholson frown and gravelly voice, "I didn't feel a [expletive-deleted] thing."

I often reflect on that scene when I look back on, and at, my life with PD. If I ever had the chance to speak with you about my thoughts on PD, I am sure that conversation would at one point or other shift to the mental aspect of PD versus its physical aspect. Having been fortunate enough to have had DBS surgery which, for me, alleviates most of the physical difficulties associated with the depletion of dopamine in my brain, I am left with focusing on how saying good-bye to dopamine means saying good-bye to what some neuro-philosophers have termed the mystery of "qualia" in the study of human consciousness.

The best way to consider what they mean by the word "qualia" is to focus on your experience of the red in a rose. Yes, it is a color by definition and can be described scientifically as a certain frequency of light. But red, as we experience it as human beings on a daily basis, is a subjective experience. You can say the same for the "smell" of fresh ground coffee in the morning and the "scents" that intertwine in our neurons to remind us of Christmas as a child. Those of us brought up on

> Saying good-bye to dopamine means saying good-bye to what some neuro-philosophers have termed the mystery of "qualia" in the study of human consciousness.

baseball can remember the "feel" and "smell" of the glove in the spring when it comes out of the closet for that first game on the newly-mown grass. Think of the multi-colored hue of the sunset in the west, as the Pacific swallows that great sphere of fire into its belly. All of these things, singularly and together, intertwine to weave the fabric of our lives on delicate neuronal looms. It is the interaction of those neurons and the subjective patterns that they create in our minds which render us, at least in my opinion, uniquely human and distinct from other species. Unfortunately for those of us with PD, the means by which those messages are tied together is through the powerful neurotransmitter, dopamine.

Dopamine is the protagonist that brings us not only movement, but the experience of life itself. Recently as I was reflecting on my lack of this powerful elixir, I realized that if one were born without dopamine, but was still by some miracle granted the power of locomotion, one would not have any ability to experience the world. No feelings, no sense of the interconnection of smells with memories, no ability to understand, ever, that simple line: "That which we call a rose by any other name would smell as sweet."

Dopamine is the protagonist that brings us not only movement, but the experience of life itself.

The world beyond the PD world has discovered this connection in spades. In October 2009 the *New York Times* had an excellent article about the "new" neurotransmitter, dopamine, and how it effects human behavior. (PD was given only a passing reference.) Books on food–behavior, sexual attraction, motivation and drive, reward-driven behavior, and even the spiritual underpinning of human nature in Dean Hammer's book *The God Gene*, have focused on the crucial role that dopamine plays in the development of human nature and character. In essence, dopamine appears to be the neurotransmitter that gives us the sense of belonging in the human group and binds us together as a part of this marvelous and mysterious experience of being.

So pardon me if I say I am a little put off about this. Being the "shake, rattle and roll" king certainly has had its drawbacks, but not being able to patch together those feelings of wonder and magic that I used to have when contemplating the universe and its wonders is really not fair. I was a music theory/composition major when I first went to university, but I barely listen to music now. Mozart doesn't move me any more, but I still wish he did. These are the things that are so difficult to describe or explain to those who struggle to understand my perspective on life as one with PD. When I say that I didn't feel anything after a particularly moving (to others) performance, they look at me as though I am not quite human. How could I not be moved to tears/laughter/ joy/sorrow, etc., as they are?

For those of you who work in the medical or research fields professionally, trust me when I say I would take the tremor back if I could just have the feeling of being human again. To look forward again to the feel and smell of baseball in the spring, to Christmas carols in December, and to sunsets in Hawaii. If I could be so bold as to suggest a marching song that can be molded to fit this request, it would be the great Irish protest song "Bread and Roses." This line appears in the chorus: "Give me bread but give me roses." For those of you out there looking for a cure for this affliction, please understand the urgency. You need to know that this man doesn't live on bread alone: the *qualia* of a rose is needed also.

> I would take the tremor back if I could just have the feeling of being human again. To look forward again to the feel and smell of baseball in the spring, to Christmas carols in December, and to sunsets in Hawaii.

In the end, perhaps the symbol for those with PD should be the Cheshire Cat that slowly fades away until nothing is left but the smile. Before that happens to me, I want the *qualia* back, if just for a time.

LODESTONES

We all at some point in life wrestle with God or his angels and find ourselves wanting. Look deeply into the eyes of people you meet to search for the signs and scars of those battles. Respect what you find there.

Take a load off. Life doesn't have to make sense.

Before beginning to think outside the box, it is best to learn how to work within it.

It's never too late at night or too early in the morning to call a parent for advice, help or just to ask a question.

LODESTONES

Check your ticket each morning. The bus idling on the curb outside is bound for parts unknown, guaranteeing new vistas, insights, opportunities, friends and an abundance of grace. If this is your morning to get on board, don't drag your heels and miss its departure.

Apologies to a friend are like vitamins to a well-watered plant: not necessary, but just watch it bloom!

LODESTONES

Spend all your life accumulating wealth and in the end you spend it all acquiring the souls and cultures of others, never having taken the time to develop your own.

At least once a year, make a detailed Stewardship List, containing all the people, places, beliefs, cultural histories, traditions, talents, and creatures (great and small) that life has entrusted to you. This list is your Life's Work. What you do for a living is only your economic contribution to this work.

Chapter 11

JOURNEY TO THE
DARK SIDE

It's twilight in the swamp. Yoda and his young apprentice are sitting around a fire contemplating the lessons of the day.

"Dreary you are this evening, young padawan. Where is your mind?"

"Sorry master Yoda, was just considering how much I would love to pass this burden of PD off on some other padawan and let them carry it a while."

"Stupid, you are. Given the gift of learning humility and humanity at an early age, you have been. See this as a gift, you must. Not otherwise. Sink in the swamp you will, Blondy, if you do not your head screwed on right get."

Before I had my DBS surgery, I had reached the point with my PD that I had what we in the know call about four hours of "on" time during the day. It's the period of time when your medications are having their best effects, and you can pass almost undetected in the general population without drawing attention to yourself as being somewhat different from the norm. Simply enough, "off" time is when your meds aren't working and all your PD symptoms return, in spades.

My four hours were usually broken up into 30 minute "on" increments, followed by 1 to 1 1/2 hour "off" increments. As a result, I would conduct all activities that needed a steady hand and body, such as washing dishes, going shopping, cleaning my apartment, working on the computer, during these fleeting "on" times. The balance of the day was spent doing my "shake, rattle and roll" routine wherever I might find myself. People with PD and those who care for them know that these transitions can be quite sudden and often quite humiliating.

I would head out to shop for groceries when I was solidly "on," and if I were lucky would make it out of the store before going into an "off" state. The most interesting part of this for me was observing the reaction to those around me. When I entered the store, I was standing tall, walking forward with purpose and conviction. I

I had what we in the know call about four hours of "on" time during the day. It's the period of time when your medications are having their best effects, and you can pass almost undetected in the general population.

was treated with the deference that "normal" people receive, as just one of the crowd.

If I went "off" before I got out of the store, I and the atmosphere around me changed dramatically. Suddenly I was hunched over my basket, my left side uncontrollably trembling, barely making progress down the isles. The same people who 30 minutes before had treated me like one of their own, now backed away from me as quickly as they could. Nobody would look me in the eye, and most considered me to be some homeless and hopeless drug addict. (I know that must be the case because of the replies I have heard parents give their children when they asked, "Mommy, what's wrong with that man?")

I morphed from a respectable citizen to a seemingly drug-crazed outcast in 30 minutes. And what could I do? Stand there in the aisle and plead with people in a shaky voice coming from a shaky body? Try to convince them that I was one of them, just experiencing the outward signs of a deficit of a primary neurotransmitter? Who is going to listen to a shaky old man begging for understanding in a grocery store? So I just passed through the register as quickly as possible and headed back to my apartment.

> I morphed from a respectable citizen to a seemingly drug-crazed outcast in 30 minutes. And what could I do? ... Who is going to listen to a shaky old man begging for understanding in a grocery store?

Now, some of you are thinking at this point that this must be the "dark side" alluded to in this chapter's title. *"Wrong are you again, young padawan."* This is the bright side of the condition, because if you can coral any of these frightened bystanders, speak to them for awhile, and explain the fundamentals of PD, they can become instantly your best and most considerate friend. Simply put, when people can *see outwardly* what the lack of dopamine in the PWP brain *inwardly* does to one, they become immediately sympathetic and kind.

(This, of course, begs the question of why they aren't that way when you are perceived as a homeless druggy. *"NOT, young padawan. The lesson learned you have not yet. That is the question answered it is."*)

What is the sympathy meter difference? Simple. Those bystanders see someone with PD or other visibly-debilitating conditions as being stricken with an unfair burden that has, by happenstance, been visited upon them. But they see homeless drug addicts as having CHOSEN their condition.

> You don't become a compulsive gambler because you want the money, you do it because you want the sweet feeling of relief that passes through your body when you get the "hit" of additional dopamine.

You cross over to the dark side with PD when the outward signs of the inner dopamine deficit are *not* the cardinal physical signs of the disorder, but the behavioral signs of the disorder. These behavioral signs include depression and apathy and, the big crowd pleasers, obsessive-compulsive disorders such as: compulsive shopping, gambling, sexual fixations, eating, etc. Because of the interaction between dopamine and the basic reward system in the brain which helps us control and modify inappropriate behavior, any activity that increases, even minimally, the production of additional dopamine in the brain, is like a healing balm to those of us with PD.

Why do these behavioral disorders manifest themselves to a greater degree in those with PD? Because of the payoff: you don't shop compulsively because you want objects, you shop compulsively because you crave the additional dopamine that this activity causes your brain to produce. You don't become a compulsive gambler because you want the money, you do it because you want the sweet feeling of relief that passes through your body when you get the "hit" of additional dopamine. Just like the heroin addict, this is the way the person with PD can get their extra "fix." (Although it's not really that simple. It's more like picking up a damp towel in the desert and wringing it out to get the last drop of moisture. You can't actually get the cells that are left to produce more, but you can add additional stress in order to wring them dry of the last drop of dopamine they are able to produce.) I know this because it was my compulsive gambling that resulted in the loss of my marriage, my children, my friends, my money, and my law practice.

There are many experiments that have been done with rats that demonstrate that the reward behavior chosen in any particular experiment is the one that involves some level of unpredictability or risk, behavior which also results in an increased level of dopamine in the brain. But it wasn't until the year 2000 that the first reports in the professional journals in Europe began to appear linking the use of some of the agonist drugs in PD patients with compulsive gambling.

From my standpoint, having been diagnosed in 1994 and having started my gambling career in earnest in 1995, this info came too late. By the fall of 2004 when I had finally faced the fact that—for whatever reason—gambling was controlling my life, it was finally being recognized as the devastating result of not only the agonist used to treat PD, but also sinemet and just PD itself. If it had not been for a friend who dragged

> It was my compulsive gambling that resulted in the loss of my marriage, my children, my friends, my money, and my law practice.

me to a Gamblers Anonymous meeting in November 2004, I am not sure where I would be today. But now, more than five years later, I have maintained my gambling "sobriety" in tact and have not placed a bet since September 27, 2004. I am still firmly of the belief that, in my case, the gambling was the result of my PD. But I am also firmly of the belief that without Gamblers Anonymous, I would not have been able to stop. Believe me, there is nothing more pitiful than seeing a middle-aged man sitting at a blackjack table (trembling so badly that no one will sit next to him) and slowly losing all of his money. Not that the casinos minded, but that is another story.

The long and short of my experience for those of you who have PD or are their caregivers or friends, is simply this: after being diagnosed with PD you hide the destructive aspects of your behavior from your doctor, spouse or friends at your *extreme* peril. PD is now not just a part of your life, it is the primary lien-holder on your body, and everything that you do must be seen in its shadow. Not all your problems can be laid at its feet, but until those problems are explored in its light, it is not safe to move on to other explanatory paradigms. This is truly the dark side of PD in my mind: the all-pervasive shadow it spreads over your entire life. It leaves no corner untouched; it takes a scorched earth policy with your soul.

And it is truly *dark* because the behavioral aspects of PD are the hardest for caregivers, spouses, children and friends to accept or to understand. Just as the people in the grocery store see the homeless drug addict as being in control of his or her choices in life, so they also see those of us with PD as being in control of our obsessive-compulsive actions. Yes, information combined with love and support can change the course of our actions, but being in control? I don't think so. That is why, I think, the Gamblers Anonymous or Alcoholics Anonymous philosophy of giving control of your life over to a higher power, however you may define that power, has such a sweeping effect. By giving up your belief in your control, you regain your sanity. By giving up your belief in your control in the right way, you can regain your humanity. By admitting

> By giving up your belief in your control, you regain your sanity. By giving up your belief in your control in the right way, you can regain your humanity.

the limitations that PD brings, you can start walking down a more pleasant path, in understanding and love.

"Depressing you are, young padawan. There is joy in finding the way back from the dark side, there is. A great strength not afforded to all beings by this journey taking. Bearing your burden with humility and peace brings great rewards, it does. So pass me another drink, young padawan, and have one yourself, do. Earned it you have."

LODESTONES

When the heart departs a relationship, it leaves no forwarding address.

Write poetry, regardless of what you think your skill level is. Doing so will teach your heart to sing.

Try to set aside a definite period of time each week in which you consciously ask and allow God to be a blessing through you to everyone with whom you come in contact. Pick the times at random, and expect the unexpected.

The trick is to learn how to be effective in the world without becoming affected by the world.

LODESTONES

You can't minister to the needs of others if your primary concern is being right.

Never forget the friends of your youth. They were each a sail that when unfurled helped speed a safe and swift passage through the straits of your heart and set the course for the rest of your life.

God is always speaking to us, but it is difficult to hear him over the cacophony created by the jackhammers, bombs, bulldozers and continual sounds of greed generated in our rush to redesign his planet in our image.

LODESTONES

There are two broad categories of friends in one's life. The first is composed of those people who add color, spice and interest and whose names may change with the seasons. The second is composed of those people who will trouble your sleep until you know they are home safely. Adding names to the first group makes your life busier. Adding names to the second group makes your life infinitely richer.

You never know you have reached your limit until you get there. You can't be sure that you are there unless you have pushed yourself. And do you ever really know whether you pushed yourself as far as you could go?

Chapter 12

ORIGINS: THE ELUSIVE MYSTERY

As I write this, I have been struggling with the worst cough/cold of my adult life the last few weeks. The symptoms are maddening: a cough that keeps me up at night; a discharge from my eyes that results in their being "glued" shut each morning when I awake; a cough so strong during the day that I become lightheaded and nearly pass out; an almost unbearable headache in the region where the wires from my DBS surgery are just underneath the skin; and a loss of focus and concentration. At least I know where it came from. Darlene had the symptoms a couple of days before I did, so I can point a finger at her and say, "It's your fault that I feel so miserable!"

The human need to cast blame for all that ails us is fulfilled. Somehow knowing whom to blame for my misery makes it more bearable, particularly when I can see that the person that I hang the guilt on is miserable too. Universal justice is fulfilled.

Of course, the search doesn't end there. Now that I have passed the buck to Darlene, she has to go one step further and find out who was kind enough to gift it to her. Because she works in a clinic, the possible villains are many, and all are readily identified in order to deflect some of my finger-pointing to those down the line.

Human beings have an innate need to find origins: whether for good fortune or bad, rain, snow or sunshine, good or bad harvests, illness or health. We won't rest until the root of our distress/good fortune is located and hardily cursed, sacrificed to or worshipped.

So it has been a frustrating and time-consuming search that I have undertaken over the last 16 years to create an origin myth for the source of my PD. How can so many (as stated earlier, estimates are 1.5 million in the United States, 4 million worldwide) have to deal with this chronic condition without someone, somewhere, knowing its origin. This is important, folks. I WANT SOMEONE TO BLAME!

> Human beings have an innate need to find origins: whether for good fortune or bad, rain, snow or sunshine, good or bad harvests, illness or health.

Somewhere down deep I feel that if I knew who did this to me, I could exact some type of revenge on the creep.

The current state of the origins search in the mystery that is PD centers on outside environmental impacts on the system. It is widely accepted by the scientific community that studies this disease that 5-10 % of the cases are genetic in origin: they are somehow inherited. The balance of 90 % or more seems to be, at this point, attributable to outside interference (although damage in some individuals may be the result of a genetic susceptibility to outside harm).

This being the case, a small minority of us with PD can blame mom and dad, and the rest of us need to look at bigger targets—such as the chemical companies. Many feel that exposure to certain pesticides is the initiating trauma that starts the disease cascade. The Food and Drug Administration (FDA) only approves chemicals by themselves, not in combination with other chemicals. Therefore a chemical approved for use by the FDA solo, could, in combination with another equally approved solo chemical, reek havoc on human beings. Other possible culprits of origin include: carbon monoxide poisoning, working around welding, severe trauma or blows to the head, and several other environmental "causes." Armed with this information, I set out to determine the possible villains in my life, those that I would need to see punished if justice were to be served.

> The scientific community that studies this disease [estimates] that 5-10 % of the cases are genetic... The balance of 90 % or more seems to be, at this point, attributable to outside interference.

Initially, I had to rule out mom and dad, as there was no history of PD on either side of my family tree. In fact, all my parents, grandparents, etc. lived well beyond their life expectancies. For two generations back at least all survived into their late 80's or early 90's. However, my father's career offered an avenue for exploration. He worked for the Agricultural Research Service of the United States Department of Agriculture for over 40 years. Because of this, we lived on or near (or visited on a regular basis) numerous agricultural experiment stations in Texas and Colorado. I spent time on those facilities as a child visiting my father, living in the midst of them, or in my teens visiting them with a .22 to hunt for rabbits. BINGO! I CAN BLAME MY FATHER, THE PESTICIDE MANUFACTURERS, THE GOVERNMENT, and GUNS. And if that isn't good enough, I had a concussion when I was 9 years old playing football, SO I CAN BLAME FOOTBALL, TOO. Just wait until I present this smorgasbord to a good personal injury lawyer. SUE THEM ALL.

This very "Old Testament" view of origins (the Christian memes of my childhood will always and everywhere color my life, its course, and its end) is somehow comforting to me. God (via the legal system) will exact punishment on the transgressors—those that released this plague on humanity—and I can get comfort in his visiting punishment on the responsible party and his children, his grandchildren, and his great-grandchildren, etc.

Or I can take the New Testament approach to origins, where the disciples in addressing a man's blindness (paraphrasing John 9:2) asked: "Is it his parents fault or his own that he is the way that he is?" Christ absolves both the parents and the man, saying it is not their fault, and heals him. In doing so, he foregoes revenge as the source for origin stories and proclaims resolution, reconciliation, healing, forgiveness and redemption as the message for the future. You can blame and stay stuck in the past, or you can forgive and resolve and move forward to the future. (Perhaps why I didn't pursue Plaintiff's Personal Injury work in my law practice. Forgiveness is not conducive to big verdicts.)

Realistically, my search for the origins of my PD has been all about blame, not truly a search for its cause and possible cure. If that had been my true motive, I could have spent the last 16 years getting a degree in biochemistry or genetics or neurology, really looking for origins with the true purpose of that search being the elimination of PD for future generations. My search is personal and reeks of revenge, a revenge that the New Testament tells me will have to be foregone if I want to accept the privilege of forgiveness and reconciliation.

LODESTONES

Life apart from God is simply a dreary exercise in statistics.

If you wake up one morning and your life feels empty and you feel a void in your heart, do an inventory of the doors and windows to your soul. The first thing you will notice is that all the locks are on the inside.

Strive to be precise, not prolific.

Try to live your life in such a manner that when you die, you are running on fumes.

LODESTONES

The same wind can either lift you up or destroy you.
It all depends on the attitude of your wings.

The most demanding task in maintaining a pluralistic
society is drawing the line between "tolerance of"
and "capitulation to."

Wisdom is purchased at a great price both to yourself
and to others. That is why her siblings are named
Humility and Sorrow.

Lodestones

If you equate "abundance" with "creature comforts," you will overlook the most fulfilling aspects of being alive.

Someday you won't be able to dance: do it now.

Always reach down to help pull someone up. Never reach up to pull someone down.

Chapter 13

THE POLITICS OF PARKINSON'S

As I write this, the United States House of Representatives is gathering to vote on the Senate's Health Care Reform bill. As a person whose life centers around health care concerns, including pricing and availability of prescription drugs, availability and competency of primary care and specialty care physicians, and availability and effectiveness of end of life care, I have plenty of skin in this game. But I am not here to argue pro or con or to take sides politically on issues such as these. What I feel compelled to address, however, is the tone of the debate and what it implies to those of us who bear the burden of PD or any other chronic neurological illness (as patients, caregivers, or family members).

At a rally concerning the Health Care bill, a proponent of the bill who had Parkinson's carried a sign that read: "Got Parkinson's? I do and you might. Thanks for your help."

The man drifted over to the group of people who were gathered to oppose the bill. The videotape of the confrontation that ensued was frightening. One of the members of the opposition group who was clearly able to read this gentleman's sign, leaned over to get directly into his face and say: "If you're looking for a handout, you're in the wrong part of town. Nothing for free. You have to work for everything you get."

At a rally concerning the Health Care bill, a proponent of the bill who had Parkinson's carried a sign that read: "Got Parkinson's? I do and you might. Thanks for your help."

One of the opposition proponent's fellow protesters followed that outbreak with one of his own, throwing a dollar bill into the face of the man with Parkinson's and saying: "Start a pot. I'll pay for you. I'll decide when to give you money."

Two things that immediately struck me were: first, the man with Parkinson's was not asking for money (for all we know he could have been a relative of Sam Walton who likes to dress like us ordinary folks and not appear ostentatious about his wealth in public). And second, he was just stating the facts: that he has Parkinson's and that some of the people whose attention he sought might have it also. (Given the current science that indicates the trauma which starts the loss of dopamine cascade, resulting in outward symptomatic evidence, begins 10 to 15 years prior to diagnoses, that was likely.) The fact that he was *for* the Health Care bill was secondary to those two points.

Then the thought swept over me that these two individuals, and perhaps hundreds, thousands or millions like them, simply maintain a deep-seated hatred for those that they think are weak or somehow are a "burden" on the "able-bodied" members of our society. (Not that *are* weak, mind you, but who *appear* to be.) When did it become permissible in the United States to throw under the bus those who are perceived as being disabled or limited in their ability to contribute to their own needs and carry their own burdens?

Taking this thought one step further, it occurred to me that the group with which the hecklers were affiliated is one that usually also takes a very strong stance for this being a country founded on a Christian and not a secular ideology. I just cannot in good conscience reconcile the thought of "Christians" looking with disdain on the less fortunate or somehow not reaching out in every way possible to help alleviate the burden, financial or otherwise, of those in ill health. The strong Christian home that I was raised in taught that the Sermon on the Mount's directions were mandatory on believers, not optional. Helping the less fortunate was the joyful obligation of those who had toward those who had not.

Current science…indicates the trauma which starts the loss of dopamine cascade, resulting in outward symptomatic evidence, begins 10 to 15 years prior to diagnoses.

Why can't our leaders, political, media and otherwise, demonstrate responsibility in this arena by reaching out to the gentleman with Parkinson's, taking him by the hand, looking him squarely in the eye and saying: "We may disagree on how to get there, my friend, but trust me that when we get to our destination, you will not be left behind." And those same leaders should then turn to the hecklers in the crowd and tell them that they are not fit for civil discussion on important adult issues and that they should go home and grow up before they participate again.

I know how dependent my Parkinson's makes me on others around me. I know that I am just one month's refill of prescription medications away from being incapable of movement, of being consigned to a wheelchair and a hospital bed, and of being totally cut off from social contact with my fellow man. And I know that those similarly afflicted with PD or other chronic illnesses are equally dependent. I also know that, in the end, it was the fault of none of us that this dependency came about.

I have what I call the "Gunfighter's Theory" of why PD seems to have blossomed in the late 20th century in the United States and throughout the world. One hundred forty years ago, if you were a gunfighter in the old west, the minute you lost a modicum of speed on the draw or your gun shook in your hand the slightest bit, you were dead. No one questioned why you were slow that day or why that day, of all days, your gun was shaking a bit and your accuracy was therefore impaired. Likewise, if you worked in the fields around dangerous machinery, when your body was out of balance and you fell into the thresher and came out bundled as wheat, no one suspected a neurological illness. Instead they would sadly declare that on that day "poor Judd was clumsy." In bygone epochs and environments, many were winnowed out by profession and didn't live to an age where neurological damage could be seen.

We live in a new age now, an age where my life expectancy will not necessarily be shortened, but my life activities certainly will be. And for those of us with young onset PD, diagnosed before age 50, the expenses of the illness will eat into any preparations we made for the latter part of our lives long before our lives are over. We will, of necessity, be obliged to rely on the kindness and strength of those not similarly afflicted. I simply hope that those in whose care our broken bodies will be entrusted have truly been instructed in the Christian underpinnings of this great nation instead of the selfish "not in my backyard" ethos of those who would walk over the bodies of the less privileged to make it into their notion of the Promised Land.

In the end, when I run into those hecklers later in life— when their bodies have betrayed them and they look to others

> I am just one month's refill of prescription medications away from being incapable of movement, of being consigned to a wheelchair and a hospital bed, and of being totally cut off from social contact with my fellow man.

to help them through the day—I hope I will still be there to lend a helping hand and to tell them that there is a seat on my bus with their name on it.

———————————

Since writing the first part of this chapter, the gentleman who threw money at the man with PD has come forward, deeply ashamed of himself, and sought forgiveness for his conduct. It is heartening to me to see this response of shame, something we seem to have forgotten in our present society. Shame is a healthy reconciler of misdeeds, and in the context in which it was expressed here, it was most appropriate. Granted, shame can be used to destroy a person, but in healthy doses it is what rehabilitates a person and allows him or her reconciliation. This gentleman indicated that as a part of his public penance he has donated money to a Parkinson's organization. As someone who was deeply offended by his original actions, (the actions probably of an individual taken up by a crowd, not the individual's better nature), I am satisfied and heartened by his response. He is welcome on my bus any time.

It should also be noted that it has subsequently been learned that the man with the sign who had Parkinson's is a nuclear engineer. He was one who did, I am sure, over the course of his working life, everything he was "supposed" to do in order to make sure that he was not a "burden" on his fellow man. I assure you he is not a burden to me.

LODESTONES

Do not unleash ideas that have no master. Likewise, do not create what you cannot contain.

When a community is in crisis, focus on the similarities and common goals of its members to help unite it, not the differences between its members to further divide it. Through this struggle to find common ground, your adversary can once again become your neighbor, and his/her differences can become strengths upon which reconciliation can be founded.

Learn to find the mysterious even in the mundane.

LODESTONES

Statistics can never tell you *why*.

When you dust your shelves, don't forget to dust your mind also.

"Stewardship of" does not imply "license to."

If you don't affirmatively choose the life you want to lead, be assured that others will choose it for you.

Don't let the ego of your youth pack in what the body of your old age can't pack out.

LODESTONES

If the world will not modify its pace to meet your limitations, then you must strive to modify your limitations to meet the world's pace.

The table has been set and the banquet prepared for eons. If we starve, it is our own choice to do so.

Life is a verb, not a noun.

There can never be peace on earth until there is peace in your own heart. Think local.

Chapter 14

THE ROAD AHEAD

In 1950 Margaret Wise Brown, a prolific children's book writer, released a title called *The Dark Wood of the Golden Birds*. I was born in 1951 and this book was in my home, so its images became a part of my early year's lexicon.

The story centers around two children, a boy and a girl, who live on the edge of a deep, dark forest with their elderly grandfather, a farmer, who dutifully tends his asparagus fields. In the dark woods live beautiful golden birds, whose songs are admired by all and whose melodies draw people from miles around to hear them. People sometimes wander into the woods unintentionally or go in purposefully to find out what they contain, but none ever return to tell their tale.

As the story progresses, there comes a time when the golden birds, for some unknown reason, cease to sing. The woods grow darker, the asparagus fields dry up, and the old man grows weak and loses his interest in life, not even rising from his bed in the morning. The young boy decides that he will go into the dark woods to discover the reason that the golden birds no longer sing.

He leaves early one morning, saying good-bye to the little girl and the old man, both of whom warn him than none that go into the dark woods ever return. Made of sterner stuff, the boy walks into the woods.

Many days pass, and the boy does not return. The birds do not sing, the old man grows older and more feeble, the crops continue to dry up, the people suffer. Then one morning, all wake to the sound of the golden birds, whose songs light up the morning sky as before. The old man awakes with a twinkle in his eye and begins to work his asparagus fields, the people are happy, all is well in the land once again. And the little girl, going out into the field that morning sees the little boy there, very quiet and pensive, working in the field tending the vegetables. He will not speak to her and has a faraway look in his eye. She approaches him carefully and will go no closer when she sees his shirt open and a golden feather piercing his heart.

The boy never speaks of his time in the woods, the birds continue to sing, and life is beautiful in the valley once again.

This book touched my heart very deeply when I first read it, and as I have aged, walking with my PD and what it means to me every day, I often think of it and its deeper meanings.

All of us with PD or any chronic life-limiting condition know what it means to venture into the dark woods. There is no guarantee that we will return, and there is certainly no guarantee that we will be healed but, assuredly, there is a promise that we will be changed forever.

I no longer look at people whom our society labels as being "disabled" as anything less than heroes who struggle each day with their various limitations, with as much dignity and strength as they can muster. There is a quiet beauty there that speaks brightly of the dignity of all life, the joy of all existence, the strength of renewed hope, and the dawn of a new day.

I have lived with PD for 16 years now and, based on current research, the initial trauma that began the cascade of cell loss in my *Substantia Nigra* probably began 10 to 15 years prior to that. So, one way or the other, my journey with PD has taken up more than half of my lifetime and all of my productive, adult life. Because of that, I see the road ahead through a different set of glasses than most.

> I no longer look at people whom our society labels as being "disabled" as anything less than heroes who struggle each day with their various limitations, with as much dignity and strength as they can muster.

I don't, however, stop to mourn the loss of what will not be. Instead, I try to focus on the beauty that is still there, the friendships that have lasted, the friendships yet to come. I try to focus on bringing out of the dark woods the lessons that I learned there, in the hope that others can find reconciliation with their body's betrayal of early, bright promise and can find comfort in the strength and meaning that their struggle can provide to even those who naively believe that their body will never betray them.

I am constantly drawn to the memes of my youth, cast in tones of judgment, redemption and reconciliation, as I have come to understand the beauty, comfort and strength to be drawn from the deep wells of Christianity. It is my fervent hope and prayer that those who grew up with memes different from mine can find the common stream that I believe waters all faith, all hope, all beauty in life.

For those who struggle with PD, all I can say about my journey to this point is that there is still abundant joy, grace and consolation to be found: the mine is just deeper and hauling the gold into the light of day takes a bit longer.

I don't, however, stop to mourn the loss of what will not be. Instead, I try to focus on the beauty that is still there, the friendships that have lasted, the friendships yet to come.

For those who care for someone with PD, try to be a patient, positive companion. I know that it is hard.

For those who neither have PD nor care for someone with it but labor under the illusion that you are bulletproof, I hope that someone will be there for you when your illusions are stripped away and life in all its glorious mystery and wonder is finally revealed.

LODESTONES

Truth is not illusive, it is usually just inconvenient.

Abandoning a project because it can't be finished in your own lifetime is the height of narcissism. Planting seeds of projects that cannot be finished in your lifetime is the essence of community.

True gifts arrive with no burdens attached.

When you get to be a grandfather, bake cookies for/ with your grandson at least once.

Any "truth" accessible only to an elite is not the Truth; it is merely a conceit.

LODESTONES

The darkness that surrounds you in the universe is stagnant. The light in the universe is dynamic and will travel billions of light years to seek you out.

The root of the joy found in every gardener's heart is the ability to see a garden in a handful of seeds.

The sea can't give back the footprints it has washed away, but neither can it stop the same pair of feet from walking there again.

We don't discover our soul by the methods of science, mathematics, philosophy or theology. We discover it when it is touched by the hand of God.

ACKNOWLEDGMENTS

The neurological and neurosurgical team at UCSF Medical Center, in particular Dr. Philip A. Starr; Dr. Jill Ostrem; surgical nurse and programmer Monica Volz;

Medtronics, for the hardware;

Dr. John A. Schafer;

My friends at PANC [Parkinson's Association of Northern California];

Those who were injured in the process of my learning many of the lessons set out here are legion, all I can hope is that they can accept my apologies and learn the lessons of forgiveness;

My Education For Ministries group at Trinity Cathedral, Sacramento, for providing shelter from the storm; hats for my newly-wired head; and hope for my heart; [and particularly for Carolyn who took me to San Francisco when it was time to turn my battery on, and Susan who helped me explore the new life that DBS provided for me];

My priest, confessor, friend, the Reverend James Richardson, and his wife and much better half Lori Korleski Richardson;

My brother Joe and sister Janice, who not only know what a family is, but also know what a family does, and do it well;

Mark Valen, for giving me a second chance;

Bill and Kathy Storey, for the ride to San Francisco, and the best example of good Samaritans that I have ever known;

Dena and Bill Freeman for the ride back from San Francisco and the opportunity to recover in the company of friends;

My daughters Tiffany and Courtney, and grandsons Gear and Dylan, who, try as I might, I cannot find adequate words to express to them what they mean to me;

Jim Hill, for being a lifelong definition of the word friend;

Akua;

And most especially to Darlene, who late in life has taught me the true meaning of the word *love*.

Keep the Cookie Pig full.